Wenceslas

Bob Chilcott

for mezzo-soprano and baritone soloists, SATB chorus, and piano or orchestra

Vocal score

MUSIC DEPARTMENT

OXFORD
UNIVERSITY PRESS

OXFORD
UNIVERSITY PRESS

Great Clarendon Street, Oxford OX2 6DP,
United Kingdom

Oxford University Press is a department of the University of Oxford.
It furthers the University's objective of excellence in research, scholarship,
and education by publishing worldwide. Oxford is a registered trade mark of
Oxford University Press in the UK and in certain other countries

ISBN 978-0-19-340476-2

Music origination by Enigma Music Production Services, Amersham, Bucks.
Printed in Great Britain on acid-free paper by
Halstan & Co. Ltd, Amersham, Bucks.

Contents

Composer's note

Written for the 150th anniversary of the iconic John Lewis store in Oxford Street, London, *Wenceslas* recalls through the poetic text by Charles Bennett the tenth-century Czech legend of a good king and his page. These two characters, here taking the form of baritone and mezzo-soprano soloists, brave the winter weather on St Stephen's Night to give a poor man shelter. The piece is through-composed, but movements 4 and 7, originally written as orchestral interludes, can be omitted if the piece is performed with piano accompaniment. Similarly, wide chords in the piano part may be spread where necessary.

Wenceslas makes use of the well-known carol 'Good King Wenceslas', spreading the five verses of text by J. M. Neale (1818–66) over several movements, and the melody 'Tempus adest floridum' (from *Piae Cantiones* 1582) appears in both original and altered forms.

Duration: *c*.24 minutes

An accompaniment for orchestra (2 fl, 2 ob, 2 cl, 2 bsn, 2 hn, 2 tpt, timp, 2 perc, hp, str) is available on hire/rental from the publisher or appropriate agent.

Commissioned by John Lewis to celebrate the 150th anniversary of the founding of the business in 1864, for first performance at the Royal Albert Hall on 1 December 2014, performed by the John Lewis Partnership's own choirs and orchestra, conducted by Manvinder Rattan.

Choirs of the John Lewis Partnership Music Society:

Voices in Partnership
The Cavendish Singers
The Lunchtime Choir
A Choired Taste
Cambridge Capella
Auld Reekie
Côr Alaw'r Fenai
Tartan Tones
Croydon Counterpoint
Junction 4
Thames Valley Voices

with

The Cavendish Ensemble

Wenceslas

Charles Bennett (b. 1954)

BOB CHILCOTT

1. Wintertide

Printed in Great Britain

OXFORD UNIVERSITY PRESS, MUSIC DEPARTMENT, GREAT CLARENDON STREET, OXFORD OX2 6DP

2. Who can that be?

Lyrics (measures 29–37):

see if we can make things bright on Ste-phen's Night for cha - ri - ty, for cha - ri - ty.

PAGE (measures 38–):
There's a man in the snow, a man in the snow with

WENCESLAS:
There's a man in the snow with

T./B. *unis.* *p*
'Hi - ther, page, and stand by me, If

attacca

3. Forth they went

We'll take a blan - ket soft and warm _____ to

wrap him up__ a-gainst the storm. _____

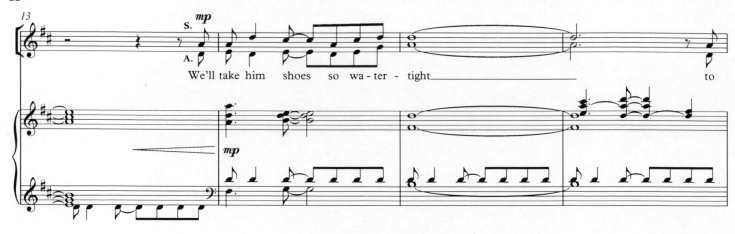

13

S.
A.

We'll take him shoes so wa-ter-tight_____ to

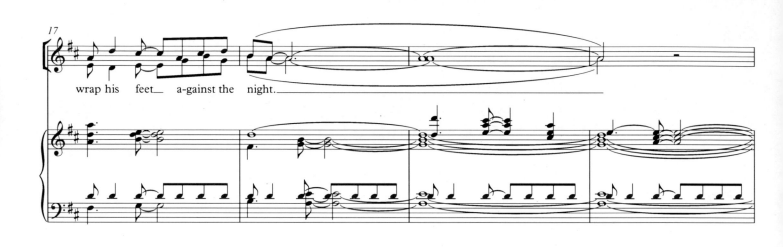

17

wrap his feet__ a-gainst the night._____

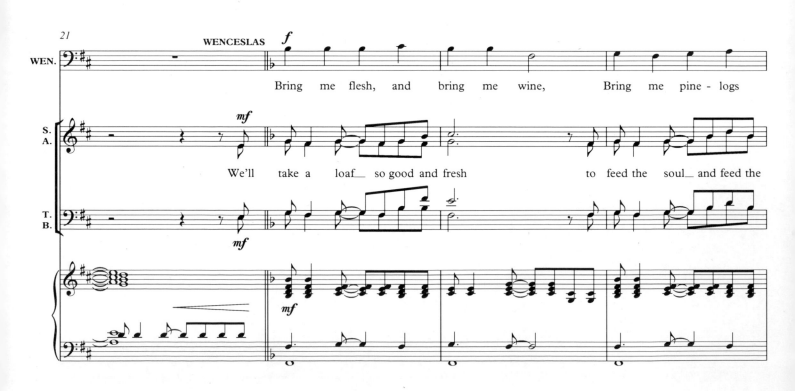

21

WEN.

WENCESLAS *f*

Bring me flesh, and bring me wine, Bring me pine - logs

S.
A.

We'll take a loaf__ so good and fresh to feed the soul__ and feed the

T.
B.

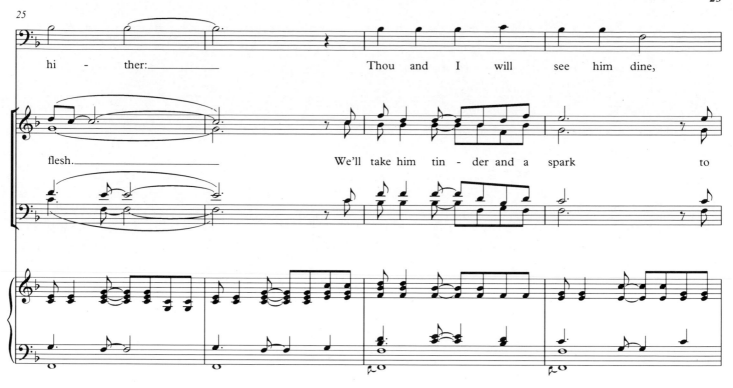

hi - ther:_____ Thou and I will see him dine,

flesh._____ We'll take him tin - der and a spark to

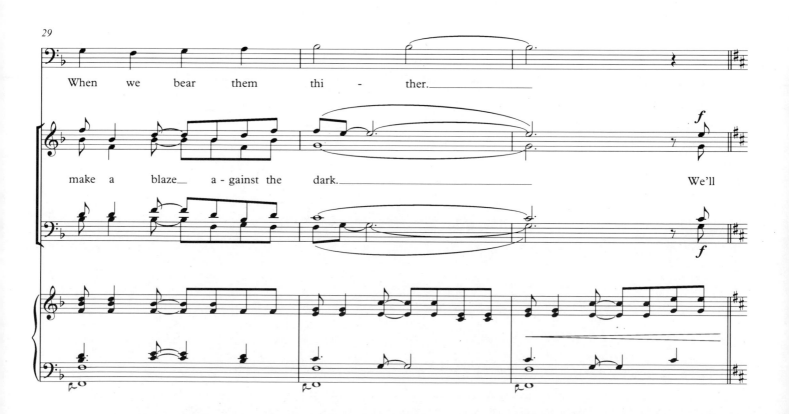

When we bear them thi - ther._____

make a blaze__ a - gainst the dark._____ We'll

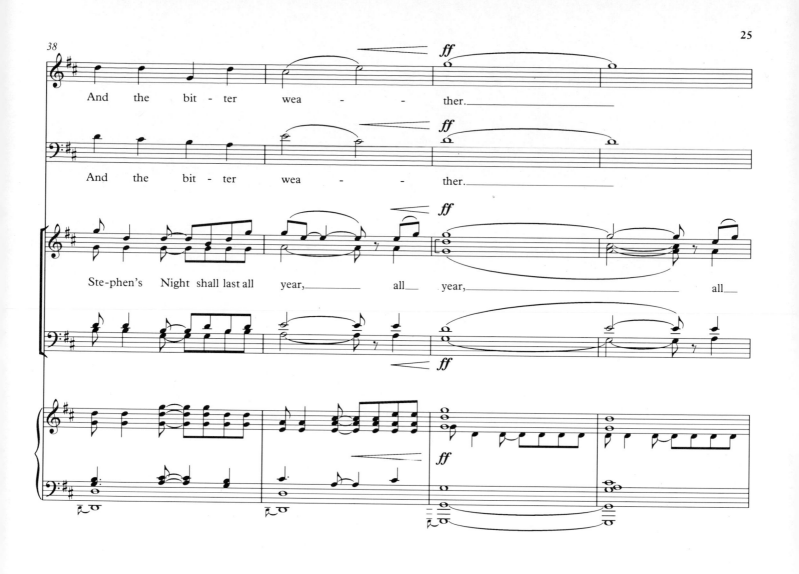

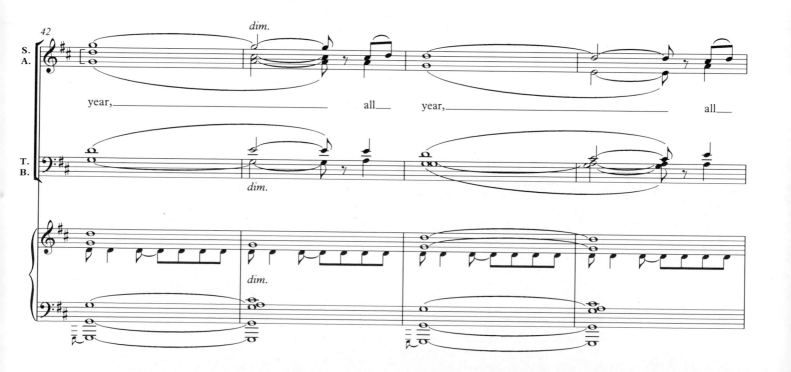

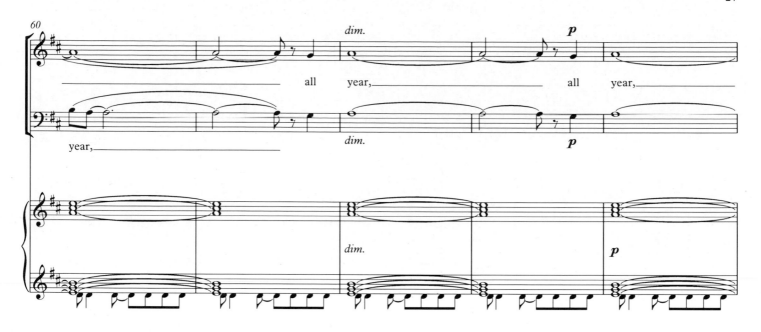

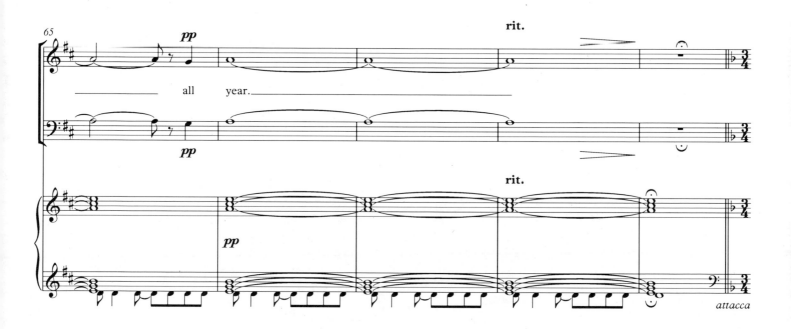

4. Interlude — Winter Dark

attacca

5. Sleeping in winter's arms

I can go no long - er.

know not how, no long - er.

no long - er.

WENCESLAS

Mark my foot - steps, good my page; Tread thou in them bold - ly:

Thou shalt find the win - ter's rage Freeze thy blood less cold - ly.

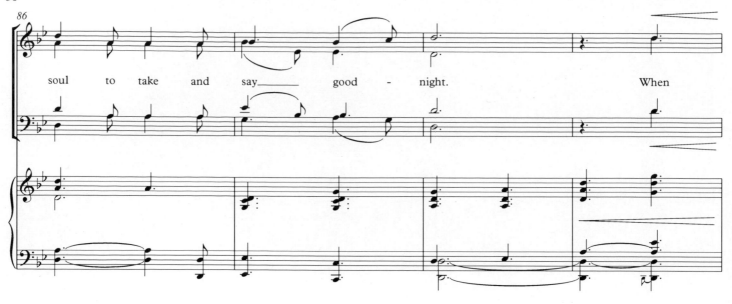

soul to take and say_____ good - night. When

PAGE

Sire, the night is dark - er now, And the

WENCESLAS

Mark my foot - steps, good my page;_____ Tread thou in them

all's said and done and i - ci - cles_____ come to freeze my_____

sleep - ing in win - ter's

arms,_____

sleep - ing in win - ter's arms.

Slow ♩ = c.58

attacca

6. Thank you

1. Ne-ver thought I'd make it this far,__ Bless my luck - y star.
2. Ne-ver thought I'd find__ the time_ to give you all that's mine.

Did-n't think I could feel a - ny-thing this real.____
Did-n't think I'd lose my fear. You made it dis - ap - pear.____

Ne-ver thought I'd find my-self here___ at the end of a-no - ther year.
Ne-ver thought we'd come that close.___ It hap-pens, I sup-pose.

Did-n't think that this could come true.___ Thank you,___ thank you.___ } For what-
Did-n't think I'd lose___ my fear.___ You made it___ dis-ap-pear.___

PAGE - ev - er you've been told, young or old, it's time to come in from the cold.___ For what-

S. Young or___ old,

A. *oo*

T. B. *oo*

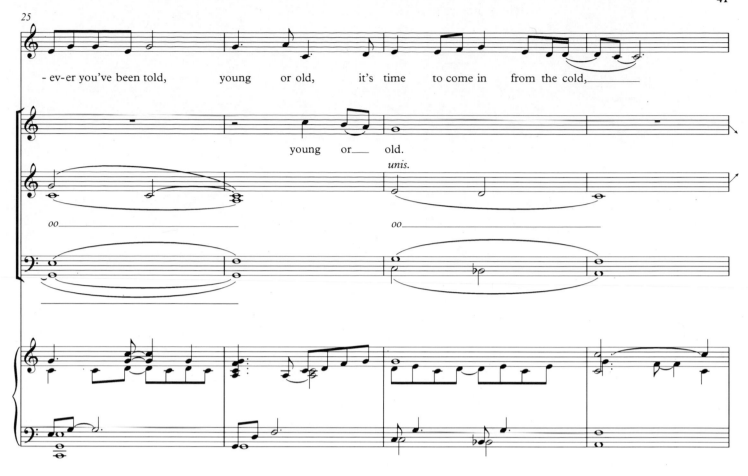

-ev-er you've been told, young or old, it's time to come in from the cold,

young or old.

unis.

oo_____ oo_____

PAGE

1. in_____ from the cold._____

2. in_____ from the cold._____

S. A.

In_____ from the cold._____

T. B.

Ne-ver thought I'd touch the sky. How sur-prised am I?

Did-n't think that dreams come true. Thank you, thank you.

Ne-ver thought I'd find my-self here at the end of a-no - ther year.___

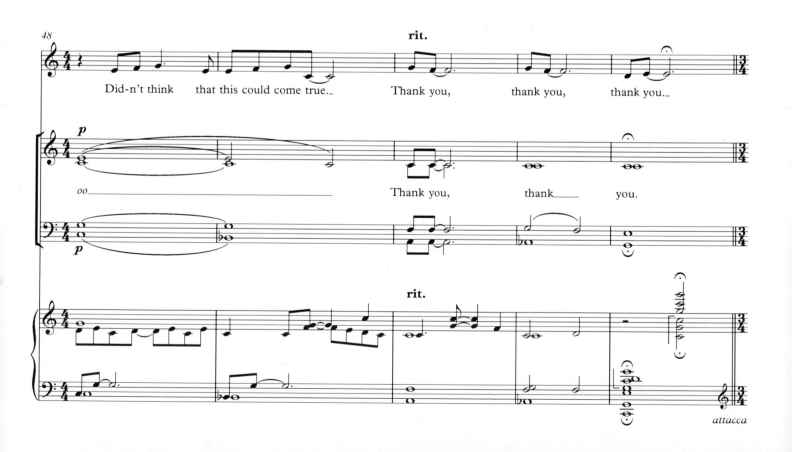

Did-n't think that this could come true._ Thank you, thank you, thank you._

*oo*_____ Thank you, thank___ you.

attacca

7. Fanfare — Winter Bright

attacca

8. On Saint Stephen's Night

burn - ing, burn - ing on Saint Ste - phen's Night.

- ing,

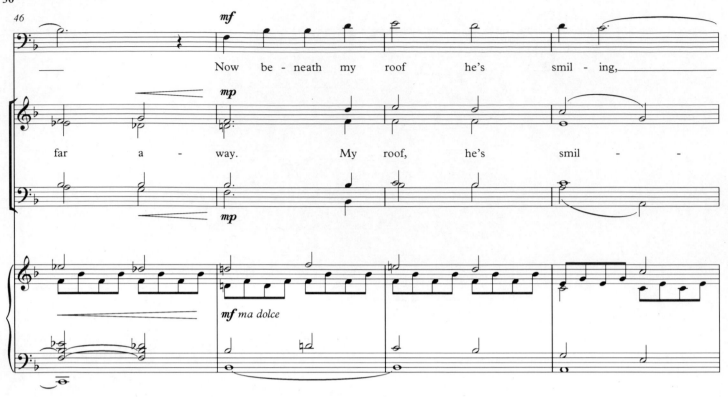

there is a King with a heart___ so warm. He

melts___ the ice and___ calms___ the storm. He

brings___ us fire and___ drink and___ food,___

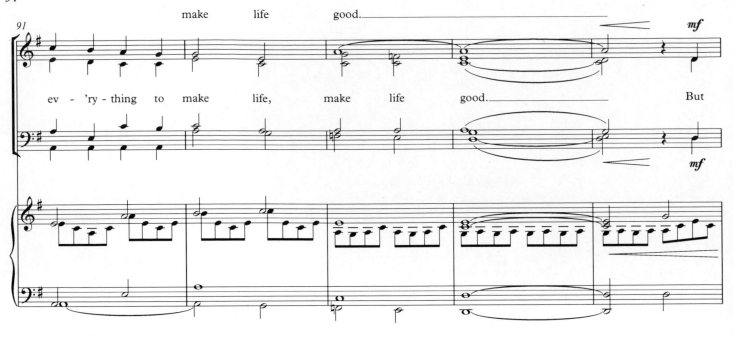

make life good.

ev - 'ry - thing to make life, make life good. But

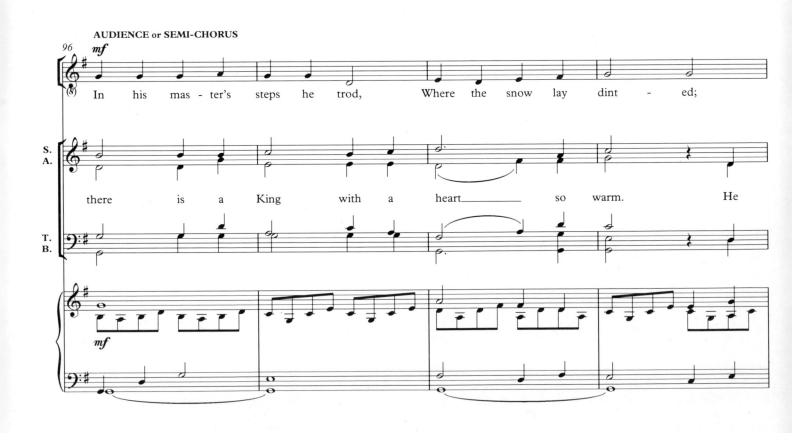

AUDIENCE or SEMI-CHORUS

In his mas - ter's steps he trod, Where the snow lay dint - ed;

there is a King with a heart so warm. He

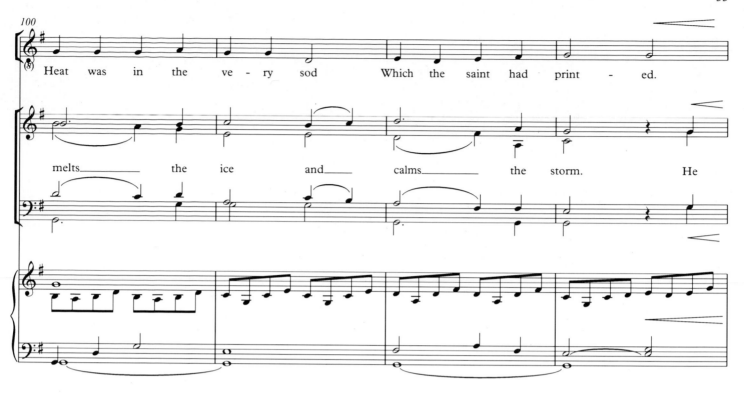

Heat was in the ve - ry sod Which the saint had print - ed.

melts_____ the ice and___ calms_____ the storm. He

There - fore, ev - 'ry - one, be sure, Wealth or rank pos - sess - ing,

brings_____ us fire and___ drink and_____ food,_____

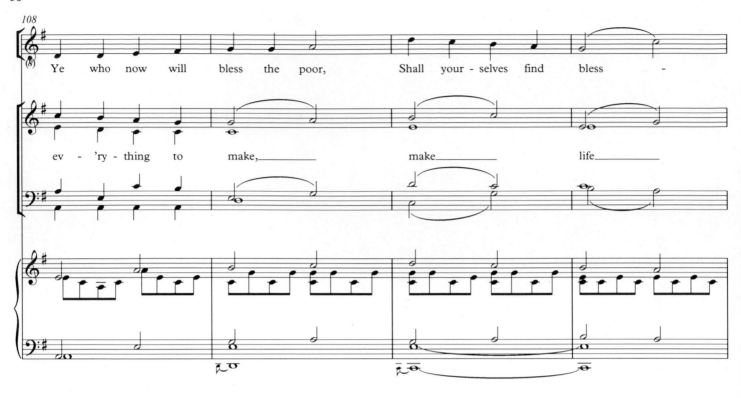

Ye who now will bless the poor, Shall your-selves find bless-

ev - 'ry - thing to make,_____ make_____ life_____

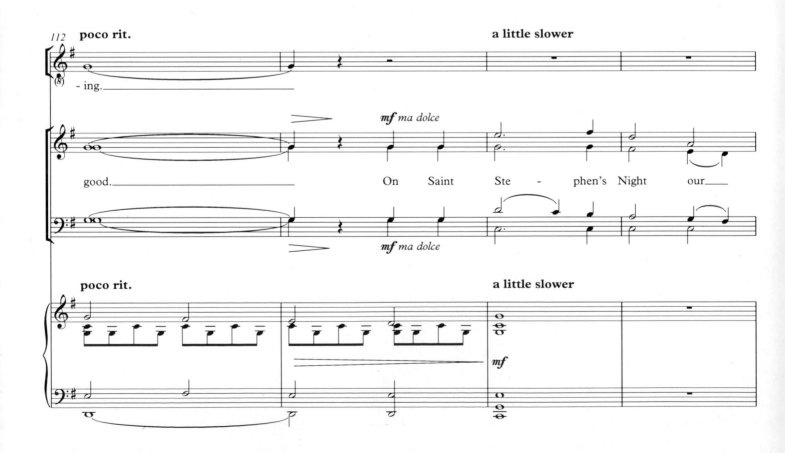

poco rit. **a little slower**

- ing._____

good._____ On Saint Ste - phen's Night our_____

mf ma dolce

mf ma dolce

poco rit. **a little slower**

mf

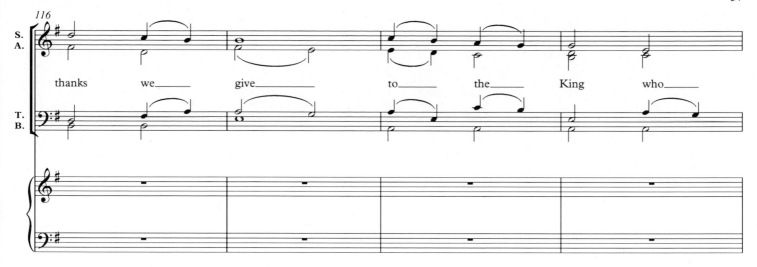

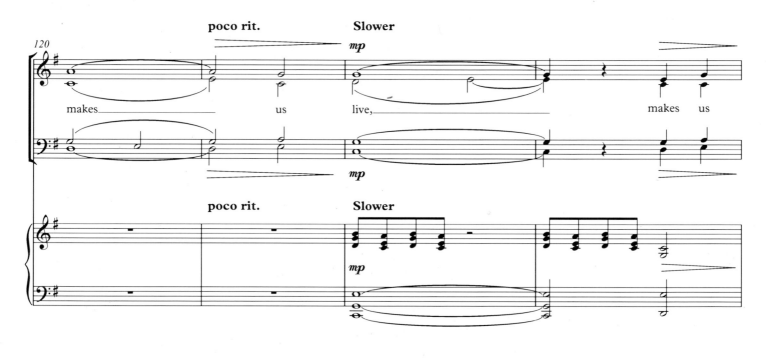

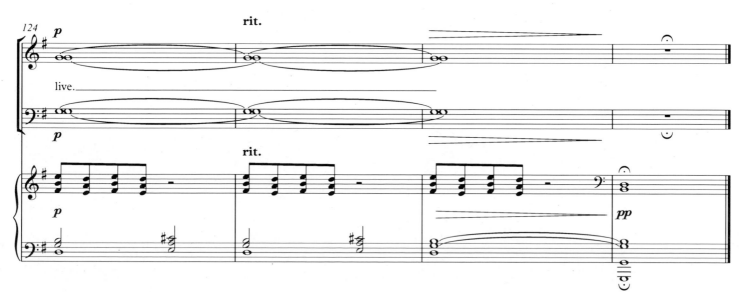

Processed in England by Enigma Music Production Services, Amersham, Bucks.
Printed in England by Halstan & Co. Ltd, Amersham, Bucks.